"'Journey' is an overused word but perhaps the best one I can find to describe *Forget Me Not*. It will likely move you in unexpected ways. Burkett will likely move you (literally) in unexpected ways. The puppets are alive. The heartbreak, when it comes, is real." —*Vancouver Sun*

"If you're someone with adventurous tastes who'd like to see what the current craze for theatrical interactivity looks like in the hands of a master . . . this show is a ceremonial experience that's very hard to capture in words." —*The Toronto Star*

"There is a great sense of ritual throughout the show, with readings of hidden letters, a footwashing ceremony, the procession, a wedding, as well as a great sense of community developed in the audience. It is beguiling, challenging and enchanting." —*Sydney Arts Guide*

"*Forget Me Not* is lively and raucous and tender and also a deeply longing work—longing for connection, for communication, for love, for safety, for ritual, for comfort. I was deep in my feelings all night afterwards . . . audience members around me shuddered and sighed like they'd just had love's first kiss. It was a wild ride that I'm glad I took." —*Mooney On Theatre*

"Burkett's energy is electric. His passion and exuberance fill the stage, encapsulating one into his visceral world. The marriage of his passion, with the stories, with the themes, and with the audience encased in a performance event, is a joy to be part of." —*Broadway World*

"Burkett is telling a story but he is also deconstructing not only the art of puppetry but also the barrier between performer and audience, and, in the process, the barriers between fellow humans. We became props, puppeteers, maestros, lighting technicians, supplicants, and all so eager to do so that we became, for the time of *Forget Me Not* and on into the rainy night, community." —*My Gay Toronto*

"*Forget Me Not* stands out most as an act of unconditional generosity . . . the chance to commune with Burkett makes *Forget Me Not* an unmissable experience." —*The Georgia Straight*

"*Forget Me Not* is a layered, interactive magic world almost too elaborate to fully picture or put into words. It's an overwhelming magical theatrical experience unlike anything else." —*Night Writes Sydney*

"A meditation on love, loss, connectivity and a heartfelt reminder of the power and symbolism of the written word." —*Limelight Magazine*

Forget Me Not

Also by Ronnie Burkett

10 Days on Earth
Billy Twinkle
Penny Plain
String Quartet
(*Tinka's New Dress*, *Street of Blood*,
Happy, and *Provenance*)

Forget Me Not

RONNIE BURKETT

Playwrights Canada Press
TORONTO

First edition: July 2022
Printed and bound in Canada by Rapido Books, Montreal

Cover and interior photos © Dahlia Katz
Author photo © John Alcorn

Playwrights Canada Press
202-269 Richmond St. W., Toronto, ON M5V 1X1
416.703.0013 | info@playwrightscanada.com | www.playwrightscanada.com

LIBRARY AND ARCHIVES CANADA CATALOGUING IN PUBLICATION
Title: Forget me not / Ronnie Burkett.
Names: Burkett, Ronnie, 1957- author.
Description: A play.
Identifiers: Canadiana (print) 20210105003 | Canadiana (ebook) 20210105038 | ISBN 9780369101570 (softcover) | ISBN 9780369101587 (PDF) | ISBN 9780369101594 (HTML) | ISBN 9780369101600 (Kindle)
Classification: LCC PS8553.U639 F67 2021 | DDC C812/.6—dc23

Playwrights Canada Press operates on land which is the ancestral home of the Anishinaabe Nations (Ojibwe / Chippewa, Odawa, Potawatomi, Algonquin, Saulteaux, Nipissing, and Mississauga), the Wendat, and the members of the Haudenosaunee Confederacy (Mohawk, Oneida, Onondaga, Cayuga, Seneca, and Tuscarora), as well as Metis and Inuit peoples. It always was and always will be Indigenous land.

We acknowledge the support of the Canada Council for the Arts, the Ontario Arts Council (OAC), Ontario Creates, and the Government of Canada for our publishing activities.

Canada Council for the Arts | Conseil des arts du Canada
ONTARIO ARTS COUNCIL
CONSEIL DES ARTS DE L'ONTARIO
an Ontario government agency
un organisme du gouvernement de l'Ontario
Canada
ONTARIO CREATES | ONTARIO CRÉATIF

For John Lambert,
who gave me the world.

Forget Me Not was commissioned by the Luminato Festival in association with Ronnie Burkett Theatre of Marionettes. The play is one of the two hundred exceptional projects funded through the Canada Council for the Arts's New Chapter program. *Forget Me Not* premiered on June 7, 2019, at the Luminato Festival, Toronto, and was later presented as part of the 2020 Sydney Festival in Sydney, Australia, by the Cultch in Vancouver, and at the Fidena Festival in Bochum, Germany, in 2022. It featured the following cast and creative team:

Created and Performed by Ronnie Burkett

Composer: John Alcorn
Stage Manager/Technical Director: Crystal Salverda
Artistic Associate, Ronnie Burkett Theatre of Marionettes: Terri Gillis
Dramaturge: Matt McGeachy
Associate Producer: John Lambert

Puppet Studio

Puppet Design and Creation: Ronnie Burkett
Costume Builder: Kim Crossley
Studio Assistants: Andy Hayward, Marcus Jamin, and Kira Duff
Shoes and Accessories: Karen Beames
Specialty Controls: Drew Lamb, Frank Meschkuleit, and Marcus Jamin

The 100 Handpuppets Project

Design Assistant/Lead Fabricator: Jesse Byiers
Assembly: Kim Crossley, Karen Beames, Thea Crawford, Sharon Gashgarian, June Gunn, Alden Hadwen, Alanna Kitson, and Deborah Lount

Scenic Elements: Hamilton Scenic Specialty
Scenic Soft Goods: Sondra Richter

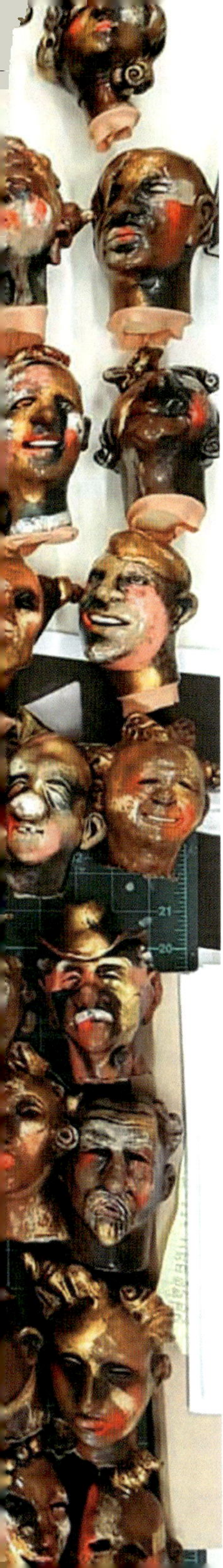

Music recorded at Desert Fish Studios
Mixing and mastering: Jeff Wolpert

Musicians

Guitar: Reg Schwager
Bass: Steve Wallace
Violin and Accordion: Drew Jurecka
Trumpet: John MacLeod
Drums and Percussion: Davide Direnzo
Keyboards and Programming: John Alcorn

Special Thanks

Josephine Ridge, Naomi Campbell, Wesley Enoch, Heather Redfern, Dina Meschkuleit, Tim Sykes, Mike Kukucska, Buddies in Bad Times, Camie Koo, Kaz Maxine, Martin Herbert, Christian Mondor, Alicia Salverda, Eva Kuo, and Chanti Laliberte.

Notes on Staging

Forget Me Not is played as an immersive experience for and with the audience. The physical playing space itself is ideally not a traditional theatre; or, rather, not a theatre environment familiar to the audience. It should create an immediate sense of mystery, and, quite possibly, some discomfort in the audience's perceptions of performance.

Such spaces might include a stage in a large, empty theatre. The audience, brought in through back hallways onto the stage, would experience the traditional performer's view of the seats in the house, all empty and illuminated by a single ghost light. A warehouse, abandoned factory, or empty building similarly would serve as a clandestine meeting place for the show about to happen in secret.

The playing area is furnished with mismatched chairs, settees, couches and benches, and worn carpets arranged in a loose circular pattern. There are several large crates, painted vibrant red, throughout the environment housing props and puppets. In the centre, a long cabinet containing marionettes on one side, handpuppets on the other. In one corner, a cabinet housing a record player sits near a lamp and wingback chair.

Overhead, the space is festooned with strands of carnival lights. Hanging by threads from and between these lights are 186 pages of yellow foolscap, each filled with cursive handwriting. These pages are the original handwritten cursive draft of the play, dancing and swaying above the audience throughout.

The audience—no more than a hundred people—will be in the playing space for the entirety of the show. When they are assembled, a voice is heard. ME, *disguised as* FALSE SHE *in a voluminous veiled and hooded robe, has been sitting stock still in a chair beside the record player.*

FALSE SHE: There once was a maiden
And she was fair.
I'm not speaking of her skin or hair,
No, her countenance, her demeanour,
That was true, beyond compare.
And yes, lovely too,
Firm and ripe and soft to touch,
Which shouldn't really matter much
Given her kindness and strength.
But this is a tale from the Long Ago
And the Once Upon a Time
When the highest currency of womanhood
Was a mine, unshafted,
And a mind free of thought—
The hows and whys—
For all that really mattered in
The Trade of the Female Sex, then and now,
Were the giggles and sighs
Between her virgin thighs
Waiting to yield and bow before
A manly god.

FALSE SHE *stands.*

If you disagree or find this odd,
Remember,
It was Long Ago and Once Upon a Time,
And yes, there was a man.
Because there is always a man
Long Ago and Once Upon a Time.
Always a man to pluck the flower,
Part the red sea, seal the deal
And drink the power of any good woman
Minding her way on his privileged path toward glory.

So yes, there is a man in my story.
But before you make up your mind that he
Was the same as all his kind,
Just another erector set unable to think outside the box,
Think again!
For he was as fair as she.

The kind of man revered by other men,
Adored by women too; mothers, maidens,
Sisters, witches, bitches, crones, shrews,

Hags, and queens, the kind of fella you'd
Bring home to dad.
And though I'm not one to spread rumours
On words untrue,
An angel and demon both whispered
That God and the Devil wanted to be him too.

He was a Knight in Shining Armor.
I shit you not, my darlings.
And not just any knight, this boy was as
Bright as the sun, the sum of all parts of
Nature's greatest beauty.

Imbued with a sense of truth,
Of right, but not righteousness,
A duty to stand firm, uphold,
And Heaven forbid or will it,
To right a wrong should he come upon it.
This was he, his pledge, his heart,
His song.

Imagine the weight of such conviction,
Such armor, such devotion,
And yet,
To hold your heart aloft,
Into the light.
Unfailing, unfaltering, never to fall.

Ah, but he did.
He fell.
The fall of man, indeed.
The only fall that causes all,
You and me, and he too,
To break faith with our creed
When a greater crusade rises in our breast.
He fell.

He fell, not down, no,
He fell up into love,
With the maiden fair.

Remember her?
She was at the beginning of my tale.
I got a bit sidetracked, admittedly,
With the knight, but c'mon, can you blame me?
You just don't meet a guy like that anymore.
But poor bastard, he was done.
There was a new Holy Grail in town.
This gal.
And of everything he knew before.
Now he knew two things more.
He was in love with a being better than he.
Sidebar—that's where the term
"Have you met my better half?" comes from, boys—
True story.

Anyway . . .
Let's get back on track,
Or rather, the path.
For this knight one day invited
His love on a walk beside the river.
And the rhythm of the water
Mirrored the rushing of his heart.
Perhaps his lust thrust somewhat
Inside his hard metal shell—
Who can know, who can tell—
But his armour could not contain his words
As his lips parted to spew
I love
I love
I love you.

Her eyes had been cast down,
As was a woman's way in
The Long Ago and the Once Upon a Time.
But she lifted her gaze to meet his,
Crossed her arms and widened her stance,
And said, "Yes, you do."
"I do what?" he asked.
"Love me," she replied.
"It's true"
"Good," she said. "It would be a pity to be in love alone."

There, in a distant wood, a dream from
The Long Ago and the Once Upon a Time,
Silent, still, save for the river's song and
The breath of two now one,
He bowed and kissed her hand.
That perfect paw, small and fair and empty.
He rose and spied his gift.
There, where river and land met,
Flowers—tiny, perfect, blue as Heaven's sky—
Beckoning him to the embankment,
Sighing, "Pick us for she who chooses you."
And he knew this was her bouquet,
Or perhaps a garland crown or two.

As he walked toward the river's edge,
She turned, asking,
"Why leave me so soon, my love?"
As he strode away, he turned his head
And over his shoulder said,
"I will never leave you."
Pointing to the patch of bluest blooms,
"Look, they grow for you, m'lady."
But he did not look, and could not see

The slope that tricked his feet,
Clad in a cumbersome suit of metal and mail,
Sliding, slipping, falling away,
Not in love, no, into the river below.
Dispatched into the drink, he began to sink,
Weighed down by armour so heavy
Not even a buoyant heart could save him.

But he was him until the end,
Noble, good, and true.
He could not swim or float or fight,
But with his hand, the drowning knight
Reached for the flowers near the shore.
Not a bunch, no funeral wreath,
One perfect posy picked.
And holding it above his head, he looked toward his love,
She, so frozen and distraught on land,
His final declaration as he met his watery grave,
A plea pledged with the flower in his hand.
For as my story ends,
From Long Ago and Once Upon a Time,
As the river bathed him in death,
Upon his life's last breath
These words were caught,
"My love, my love, Forget Me Not."

The moral of this story, if there is to be one at all, I suppose is this—don't go swimming in a suit of armour, asshole. No wonder chivalry is dead.

The costume comes off. ME *is revealed.*

ME: Hello, friends. Thank you for finding us.

Clearly I am not She who you've come to see. No, I am simply Me.

And I am but a fool. Which, in the old days, used to be a pretty good job. But now, everyone's doing it, so it's lost the cachet. Still, you know what they say—"No fool like an old fool."

I had to know that none of you were one of them, because had an Enforcer been in our midst, I as She would now be captured. Or dead. So, a test, yes. A trick, a fake out, and true, a lie. But I must protect her, above all and anyone else. She, the Keeper of the Lost Hand. Because you, the very ones she serves, are leading the Enforcers of the New Now to this place. They track your every move, every purchase, every whim, each conversation, all your vices, and every little sin. You are made devices in their hands.

Speaking of devices, silence them, ringers off. Do it, now. Silence is key, on your device as well as you. Shhh. Voice recognition. They're listening. Shhh. Trust me, this is not where you want to die. Better me than you or She.

If you have large bags or backpacks, place them there, and come back quickly. Do it, now. Clear the space of personal effects.

You will be moving around. Sometimes at will, self-adjusting your view, other times as directed. I will be moving a lot, and if you can't see, feel free to follow me.

ME indicates a basket of flashlights.

These are to share. You needn't light me, but She and the others you'll meet depend on your illumination. So, if you can't see them, grab a torch and light their way.

And finally, although I would prefer not, if you absolutely require the toilet during our sacred time, do not make a show of your business, discreetly leave there, but be aware you may be caught, killed, or worse, not allowed back in. Regardless, wash your hands.

I hate rules, I do, but they must be done. And now they are, so let's begin and have some fun. For friends, it is not as dismal and dreary as I portend, no; this is a celebration of love letters, written and read.

> ME *opens one side of the puppet crate and shows* BOY IN A MAN SUIT *and* WARRIOR GURL.

Here's a love story, already begun. Two destined to love as one. A boy, still a pup, but dressed in a man suit, armour for which he has not been groomed, merely assumed. And here, a warrior girl, the lot of youth rendered underground in our New Now, left to their own devices, alone and unplugged.

Music, please! Maestro, music! Ugh, I knew I forgot something in the rules.

> ME *hands the small marionettes to two people in the audience.*

Hold these.

> *He goes to the record player.*

You will be my maestros. Here are the records. They're in order, left to right, first to last. When asked for music, you pick up the record on the left, put it on the turntable, and place the needle, gently. When the music ends or I call for it to stop, you lift the needle, remove the record, and place it here. Simple, huh?

Who will start?

> ME *chooses someone close to the record player and hugs them.*

> ME *returns to the two people holding the marionettes and demonstrates their manipulation.*

Stand, please, and make your hand their ground on which they stand. Tilt the top bar from side to side. See, they walk. Don't let them fall, and, above all, don't drop them!

The rest of you, stand and make a path with your hands, become the bridge, the mountain they climb. Move them around on their epic journey and share them.

Maestro, music please!

Record Cue #1: Epic Journey

The puppets are moved around in opposite directions on the raised hands of the audience. They climb over backs and across outstretched arms. ME *encourages them to hand the puppets off so others can try, as the audience stands and becomes the pathway for the journey.*

The music ends. ME *takes the two puppets and returns them to the crate.*

ME: Thank you, friends. Soon, She will come, to write and read your love letters, but first you must be transformed.

ME *indicates a pathway in the playing space, leading to a crate off to the side.*

This is the path to your other self. The most exciting journey you will make tonight, and, for some, of your life. It was for me.

He takes the lid off the crate, revealing the One Hundred Handpuppets. He holds several of them up as he speaks.

These are the Others. Somebodies, nobodies, anybodies. They are yours. Not forever, just while we are together, here and now, tonight.

They will be your Other. You'll be asked to do things, and it's better to pretend and easier with them, trust me.

You are their skeleton, the life inside your Other.

He holds his index finger up.

Head.

Thumb.

Hand.

Little finger.

Hand.

Now, some prefer this . . .

Thumb and middle figure as hands.

. . . but it's lopsided.

Back to first pose.

This is better, more balanced. And aside from being spine, it's also a sign.

To crowd:

I love you.

Friends, starting there and single file, walk the path to your new self, and, in silence, prepare to receive your Other with gentle hands.

Maestro, music please!

Record Cue #2: One Hundred Puppets

ME distributes the One Hundred Handpuppets to the audience one at a time. When completed, he moves to the centre of the playing space.

ME: Study them, witness them, give them a story, a name known only to you. And when you're ready, become one and give them life. Bow to your neighbours. Shake their hand, give them a hug. And clap in delight, because now, you are not alone.

Greet one another, move about.

The audience move about and greet one another as their OTHER. ME's bare hand speaks in ZAKO's voice.

ZAKO: Excuse me.

I said excuse me. Hello?

Breaks handpuppet pose, slaps ME on the head.

ME: Ow! I'm doing a sacred ceremony here.

ZAKO: And I'm naked! Do you really want them to see my little thing?

ME's other index finger becomes the naked ZAKO's penis.

ME: Stop it!

ZAKO: You stop it!

ME: I'm not doing anything.

ZAKO: My point exactly! And the flatties and gillies are waiting for a show.

ME: The who?

ZAKO: Varda, ducky.

ZAKO indicates the audience.

ME: These are pilgrims, here for the sacred ceremonies of She.

ZAKO: These are punters, and they can't see She until they see me. I'm part of this too, remember? And do I look like the sort of joggering omee who would set his lattie on this tober just to slang for myself? Now, put on my slap and gildy clobber and let's get to work before Hilda Handcuffs raids the camp and shuts this whole thing down.

ZAKO slaps ME's head again.

Idiot.

ME: Stop it! Fine.

ME opens the centre crate, puts on a belt with hooks, and hangs handpuppets from it. He indicates for the audience to arrange themselves facing a particular direction.

Friends, please arrange yourselves facing here. If you can, sit on the floor, or on seating to the sides, or standing in the rear.

Record Cue #3: Fairground

ME: For now, before I present She, a glimpse of the past. A curtain raiser, if you will, a bit of Punch before the meal, some good, old-fashioned dolly wiggling puppenspieling.

He puts on a wearable walking puppet stage with a small proscenium.

I give you the Totally True—and I should know, I'm the one who made it up—tale from the Long Ago and the Once Upon a Time, of Zako Budaydos and His Dancing Bear!

ZAKO pops up as kazoo fanfare plays.

ZAKO: Greetings, beautiful mens and handsome ladies. I am the one and only Zako Budaydos!

Beat. ZAKO disappears, then pops back up as kazoo fanfare plays again.

The one and only Zako Budaydos! C'mon, give me a break, you guys.

ZAKO pops back down, then reappears as the kazoo fanfare plays again.

Zako Budaydos!

Satisfied with the audience response, he continues.

Thank you, my friends! Tonight, here in my humble gypsy tent, the most spectacular show you've ever seen, featuring a cast of thousands! Okay, maybe hundreds. At least a dozen. Well, a cast of . . . lots. Lots and lots of people.

NUTZO: *(off)* Boss!

ZAKO: What? Where is that strange voice coming from?

NUTZO: *(off)* It's me, boss.

ZAKO: Me who?

NUTZO: *(off)* Someone you know.

ZAKO: The voice is coming from there, down below. Who could possibly be beneath me? I must pace.

He paces, thinking.

Aha! Faceless coward beneath me, are you a critic, come to kiss my feet?

NUTZO: *(off)* No.

ZAKO: Are you a politician, come to kiss my ass?

NUTZO: *(off)* No.

ZAKO: Aha! Are you the devil, come to take my breath with your kiss of death?

NUTZO: *(off)* No!

ZAKO: Then show yourself!

NUTZO pops up.

NUTZO: It's me, boss. See?

ZAKO: Nutzo!

NUTZO: Hi, boss.

ZAKO: Mens and gentle ladies, please forgive. This is Nutzo, Nutzo Baad, my halfwitted assistant. Nutzo, why are you talking in such a strange voice?

NUTZO: I don't know. That's why I was hiding below. I think I have something stuck in my throat.

ZAKO: What did you eat?

NUTZO: I dunno.

ZAKO: What do you mean, you don't know?

NUTZO: I don't remember.

ZAKO: How can you not know what's stuck in your throat?

NUTZO: Because . . .

ZAKO: What?

NUTZO: The thing you always say.

ZAKO: Which is?

NUTZO: Nutzo, you're . . .

ZAKO: . . . an idiot!

NUTZO: Exactly.

ZAKO: Okay, what are the possibilities? Knowing you, perhaps a bit of candy?

NUTZO: Nope.

ZAKO: A stringy celery stalk?

NUTZO: Nope.

ZAKO: A little bit of cod?

NUTZO: Nope.

ZAKO: A chewy chunk of cow?

NUTZO: Nope.

ZAKO: A juicy piece of cock?

NUTZO: I think I would remember that.

ZAKO: Open your mouth . . .

NUTZO: Uh, boss?

ZAKO: So I can take a look.

NUTZO: Oh. No.

ZAKO: Why not?

NUTZO: My mouth doesn't open.

ZAKO: Then why are you always talking? There's only one thing to do!

NUTZO: Cancel the show?

ZAKO: Cancel the show? Cancel the show? We have an audience. Nutzo, how can you be . . .

NUTZO: Such an idiot?

ZAKO: At least that you remember! No, I must take matters into my own hands!

NUTZO: What are you going to do?

ZAKO: A manoeuvre.

NUTZO: A manoeuvre?

ZAKO: It's called the Hind Lick Manoeuvre.

NUTZO: Uh, what am I supposed to do?

ZAKO: Nothing, just try to relax. I'll do all the hard work.

NUTZO: I've heard that before. I don't know about the Hind Lick, boss.

ZAKO: Hey, it's no picnic for me either, pal. Now, turn around.

NUTZO: Have you done this before?

ZAKO: Nutzo, please. I'm in show business.

He puts his arms around NUTZO.

Ready?

NUTZO: Hold me, boss.

ZAKO: Nutzo, don't make this weird.

ZAKO thrusts behind NUTZO three times. On each, ZAKO grunts and NUTZO says, "Oh."

NUTZO: Oh . . .

ZAKO: Oh oh.

NUTZO: I think it just got weird.

ZAKO: But is it helping?

NUTZO: No, but suddenly I don't care.

ZAKO breaks free.

ZAKO: This will go down in the anals of medical history as a complete failure!

Nutzo, that's it!

NUTZO: Boss?

ZAKO: Go down!

NUTZO: Um . . .

ZAKO: If whatever is stuck in your throat won't come up, we'll force it down.

NUTZO: And how were you thinking of doing that, boss?

ZAKO: The old-fashioned way, Nutzo!

NUTZO: That's what I was afraid of.

ZAKO: Nutzo, you are like a brother to me.

NUTZO: Aw, thanks, boss.

ZAKO: You are my right hand, literally, my partner in crime, my compadre, my sounding board and whipping boy, and my best friend, because I don't have other friends. I only hope you can forgive me.

NUTZO: For what?

ZAKO: For this!

He lunges at NUTZO *and starts choking him.*

NUTZO: Aagh! Boss!

ZAKO *chokes* NUTZO, *and during the following, bashes him on the playboard in unison with the end of each line.*

ZAKO: Out, out, damned potted pie or spotted dick that makes this guy so sick and chirping like a bird.

NUTZO: Boss!

ZAKO: Release him, devil meat, so my ears are free from tweet, tweet, tweet.

NUTZO: Boss!

ZAKO: Be gone, I say, impure lamb or duck or ham he bit.

NUTZO: Boss!

ZAKO: And down you go to the hellish bowel pit!

NUTZO *is limp and silent.*

Nutzo? Nutzo, speak to me!

ZAKO throws himself on top of NUTZO and fake sobs. NUTZO rouses, his vocalization descending from high to low pitch.

NUTZO: Boss?

ZAKO: Nutzo!

They embrace.

Feel better?

NUTZO: Gimme a second.

He passes gas.

Better.

ZAKO: Good! Then on with the show! Nutzo, below. Go, get ready.

He pushes NUTZO down and turns to the audience.

Lady men and gentle femmes, thank you for your patience while I dealt with my underling. And now, the crown jewel of the carnival. The sassiest spectacle of the sideshow. A femme fatale from an exotic land far, far away. Sissy boys and butchy girls, I give you hanky-panky hootchie-kootchie harum scarum!

ZAKO ducks down. As kazoo music plays, NUTZO appears, disguised in belly-dance garb. His padded hips jiggle and wiggle ridiculously. Doing a backbend, the veil flips over and reveals his face.

ZAKO: *(off)* Nutzo, Nutzo! Your face.

NUTZO: What about it, boss?

ZAKO: *(off)* It's showing. Turn around! More harum, less scarum!

As NUTZO *turns around to face upstage, we see his bare buttocks.* ZAKO *pops up.*

Agh! Get off the stage, you ass!

He pushes NUTZO *down out of sight.*

It appears our femme fatale was more fatale than femme. But not to worry, ladybroads and misterhims, our next act is a daring display of . . .

A handpuppet of SHE *appears.*

SHE: Is it my turn now?

ZAKO: You?! What are you doing here?

SHE: I'm tired of waiting.

ZAKO: You're not in this part. I'm doing a show!

SHE: But they've come to see me!

ZAKO *whispers to* ME.

ZAKO: Me, get her out of here!

SHE: Who here has come for a love letter?

ZAKO: No, no, no, no! You have to go. My little show is from the Before, in the Long Ago . . .

SHE: . . . and Once Upon a Time?

ZAKO: Yes! But you are in the Now.

SHE: I need my crown. Please give it to me.

ZAKO: Not yet. That comes later.

SHE: But it's my crown.

ZAKO: True, but it was mine before I gave it to you. So, you have to wait.

SHE: I'm too old to wait.

ZAKO: Actually, you're not even born yet.

SHE: I don't understand.

ZAKO: Do you know what's down there?

SHE: Where?

ZAKO: There, below.

SHE: No. What?

ZAKO: A bear!

SHE: I like bears.

ZAKO: I know you do. Everyone else is waiting to see him too.

SHE: What should I do?

ZAKO: Why don't you watch from down there? And when I'm done, you can have your crown.

SHE: Promise?

ZAKO: Of course, it's yours after all. Now, down you go.

ZAKO helps her pop down.

Me! Stop mixing up present and past, it's confusing enough as it is.

ZAKO turns to the audience.

Heh heh heh, pardon that little pause, please. And speaking of paws, our next act is unbearably good! Nutzo, are you ready?

NUTZO: *(off)* Not really.

ZAKO: What's taking you so long?

NUTZO pops up. He's wearing a bear costume minus the head.

Nutzo, where's the head?

NUTZO: Boss, I can't see with the bear head on.

ZAKO: It'll be fine. What could possibly go wrong?

NUTZO: But, boss . . .

ZAKO pushes him down and turns to the audience.

And now, ladies and mens, childrens of all ages, I present on our little stage, a beast uncaged, to astound you!

Kazoo fanfare, ZAKO pops down. NUTZO, now disguised as a bear on a unicycle, appears. Slowly, perilously, he starts to wheel around, but as he picks up momentum rolling back and forth across the playboard the bear head spins.

NUTZO: Uh, boss . . .

ZAKO: *(off)* Keep going, you're doing great!

The unicycle becomes more frantic, frenetic, seemingly in peril of tossing NUTZO *off the edge into the audience, picking up speed.*

Nutzo, slow down. Just balance, they'll love it.

The unicycle pauses, and although the head is facing backward now, NUTZO *balances precariously. There is a kazoo fanfare as* ZAKO *pops up.*

Wonderful! Ta-da!

He throws his arms open in an expressive move, accidently knocking the unicycle, which falls backward and out of sight.

Sorry, Nutzo.

And now, in our caravan of deceits and delights, an act so bold, so chilling, so dangerous!

I will need two volunteers from the audience, please.

Two are selected.

Now, on my right, please raise your left arm high. And on my left, your right.

He reaches down and produces a rope, handing one end to each of the volunteers.

Take this rope in your Other's hands, my friend, and you, the other end. Now, pull it taut and tight and raise it right about here, under my chin. Perfect! Stay there, please.

And now, it is with the greatest pleasure and considerable trepidation, I give you, the aerial sensation of the tightrope, the Great Nutzini!

Kazoo fanfare reveals NUTZO, *who pops up dressed in a sequined costume and headband/turban concoction.*

Tonight, Nutzini will walk across this tightrope . . . blindfolded!

NUTZO: Uh, boss, you didn't mention that before . . .

ZAKO: It'll be fine! What could possibly go wrong?

ZAKO *pulls the headband down, covering* NUTZO*'s eyes.*

And now, Nutzini will climb up on the rope!

Kazoo fanfare. Beat. Nothing.

Nutzo! Get up on the rope!

NUTZO: I dunno where it is, boss.

NUTZO *blindly feels around him.*

ZAKO: Reach up. Can you feel the rope?

NUTZO *reaches up, fingertips barely touching the rope.*

NUTZO: Uh, I think it's too high, boss.

ZAKO: Come on, Nutzo, stretch!

NUTZO *stretches to no avail, then tries a few lacklustre hop jumps.*

NUTZO: I don't think I can do this, boss.

ZAKO: Ugh, of course you can. Let me give you a boost.

ZAKO puts his arms around NUTZO, face to face.

NUTZO: Um, boss?

ZAKO: Nutzo, don't make this weird.

NUTZO: You smell like goulash.

ZAKO: Thank you. And do you know what you smell like?

NUTZO: What?

ZAKO: An idiot! Okay, on the count of three. Ready?

NUTZO: Ready.

ZAKO: One . . . two . . . three!

They do this lifting schtick three times. ZAKO cannot get NUTZO off the ground.

Nutzo, you gotta cut down on the potatoes and bread.

NUTZO: Maybe it would work better from behind.

ZAKO looks out, deadpan.

ZAKO: I've created a monster. Fine.

He goes behind NUTZO and puts his arms around his waist.

Ready?

NUTZO: Go!

ZAKO: Heave-ho! And a one . . . and a two . . . and a three!

Come on, come on, you can do it.

NUTZO: No, no, no!

ZAKO: Yes, yes, yes!

NUTZO: No!

ZAKO: Let me know when you're close.

NUTZO: Oh, oh, I'm getting close.

ZAKO: Yes, that's it, come on!

NUTZO: I'm almost there!

ZAKO: Yes, yes, come on!

NUTZO: Yes! Yes! Yes!

> *NUTZO's hands are on the rope. His head flops in exhaustion as ZAKO releases him.*

ZAKO: Now, pull yourself up, sit on the rope, then you can stand.

NUTZO: Um, it's a little tight. Can I have some slack?

> *ZAKO addresses the two volunteers holding the rope.*

ZAKO: Fine! My friends, keep the height where it is, but release a bit of rope. Yes, good, a little bit more. Perfect!

Okay, Nutzo, now use your feet on the ground to give a little hop onto the rope, sit, and slowly stand.

NUTZO: Boss, I'm nervous. I can't see. What if I lose my balance?

ZAKO: Nutzo, relax. I'm here to catch you if you fall.

NUTZO: Where?

ZAKO: Right here.

NUTZO: Where's that?

ZAKO: Back here.

NUTZO: Which way is back?

ZAKO: Ugh, Nutzo, Nutzo. Behind you. Follow my voice.

NUTZO: Oh, okay, I hear you, boss. There you are.

> *As NUTZO turns, his head gets caught in the rope, strangling him. He struggles to talk.*

Uh . . . b . . . b . . . boss . . .

ZAKO: Let's get on with the show!

ZAKO walks downstage, oblivious to NUTZO's plight.

Manly shes and lady hes, thank you for your patience, once again. And now, an act that will take your breath away.

He speaks to the rope holders.

Pull the rope taut again. Make it nice and tight, please.

As they pull the slack and tighten the rope, NUTZO's now lifeless body hangs in the middle.

I give you, the Great Nutzini!

Kazoo fanfare. Beat. ZAKO looks over his shoulder, sees NUTZO, and walks over to the body.

Nutzo?

He pokes NUTZO. Beat.

Nutzo?

Pokes again. Beat.

Nutzo?

Nutzo! No! Release the rope, let it go. Look what you've done. You've killed Nutzo! Okay, technically he killed himself—because he's an idiot—but my best, and only, friend is dead.

He carries NUTZO's limp body downstage. He throws himself on top, sobbing.

Oh Nutzo, Nutzo, why did you leave me . . . before the finale. I was going to shoot you out of a canon.

ZAKO sobs, this time almost for real, as he picks up NUTZO and slowly goes below. The stage is removed, and ME goes to the centre cabinet. He produces a small handpuppet-sized coffin, opens the lid, places NUTZO inside, and closes it.

ME: I will need six pallbearers.

ME selects six from the audience.

Three on each side, please. Shoulder the casket of Nutzo Baad.

ME places the coffin in the middle of the six pallbearer puppets, adjusting them gently as needed.

Maestro, music, please.

Record Cue #4: Funeral

ME: Please let your Others rise and join the procession as Nutzo Baad makes his final journey from the stage to the grave.

ME leads the pallbearers around the space in time to the music. The rest of the audience walk slowly behind them, Others held high. When they reach the One Hundred Handpuppets crate, ME takes the coffin from the pallbearers and places it inside. He hugs each of the pallbearers and turns to the crowd.

Friends, be seated. She is coming now.

The stage manager puts a record on.

Record Cue #5: The Entrance

SHE enters, a tiny marionette, dressed only in a slip.

SHE: Underwear is overrated.
Nonsensical, too.
A cotton catch-all for the final drips,
Satin if you're lucky,
Or plucky,
Hoping for a little fucky.
Horsehair if you're a priest,
Which is bullshit, to say the least.
It rubs me the wrong way;
The men of the cloth, not the weave itself.
The desired is not accountable to the fetishist.
Why blame a horse for the fanaticism of
God's raping storm troopers?
A horse can shit while walking,
A priest, only when he's talking.

Liberate your loins!
Air out your sacred holes,
They might enjoy the breeze after
Squeezing out the waste of you.
What twats we mortals be
To think a lacy brief masks the
Beautiful horror of pudendum.
Why gag the shrieking vulva and
Braying gonads with a veil
When their song is the very stuff of life.
Unstuff your stuff and breathe!

I do like a slip, though.
A bit of silky nonsense lingering on my skin.
Flicking my ancient nipples with a

Teasing caress like a schoolboy's tongue,
Brushing my withered bush like
A lecher in the pew.
A slip is enough on its own,
Yet oft relegated to the role of intermediary,
To barter between frock and crack,
Skirt and thigh,
Blouse and back.
I eschew the common dress,
Your zippers, buttons, and seams,
Unbind my disappointed tits and free my beaten yoni
To dance in their own delight under the
Soft, swaying, whispering
Canopy of cloth.
Slip, slip, slip
I am slipping away.

Hello, darlings. Let's write some love letters!

You know, people always ask me, "When did you write your first love letter?"

> *SHE selects someone and stands on their hand.*

Honey, hold me, and I'll tell you the story.

> *ME hands SHE's marionette control to the selected audience member.*

Don't let me slump, or float, or fall. And above all, don't fuck around.

> *ME leaves them, gets two small marionettes, one of SHE as a young woman and the other a handsome young man, HE, holding a letter in his hand. ME whispers to two patrons seated beside one another to hold their hands out, palms up. The marionettes stand and sit on their palms.*

HE: Hello.

YOUNG SHE: Hello.

HE: I got your letter.

YOUNG SHE: Good.

HE: Yes, very.

YOUNG SHE: Really?

HE: It's wonderful.

YOUNG SHE: Oh, I was so worried.

HE: So beautiful.

YOUNG SHE: You too.

HE: The letter.

YOUNG SHE: Oh.

HE: You know so many words.

YOUNG SHE: Sometimes it's hard to find the right ones, to know what to say.

HE: I think you found the right ones this time. I love them.

YOUNG SHE: Me too.

HE: I was wondering . . .

YOUNG SHE: Yes?

HE: Will you write one for me?

YOUNG SHE: That one is for you. You didn't know?

HE: Yes. But no, not another one to me. One for someone else. From me.

YOUNG SHE: Me?

HE: Yes. Maybe you could write one like this. I'll pay you.

YOUNG SHE: I don't understand.

HE: I don't have your words.

YOUNG SHE: You don't need my words. Use yours. They'll mean more.

HE: I don't know how.

YOUNG SHE: Just write what's in your heart.

HE: But your hand is better. Look how beautiful.

HE holds the letter up.

Perfectly joined. Reading your letter made me realize how I've been feeling.

YOUNG SHE: So, you feel the same way too?

HE: Deeply. And I want to tell her.

YOUNG SHE: Then just tell me.

HE: She's wonderful. You'd like her.

YOUNG SHE: Her?

HE: My love. She's beautiful.

YOUNG SHE: Of course she is.

HE: So you'll help me tell her?

YOUNG SHE: No.

HE: But you must.

YOUNG SHE: Why must I?

HE: Because you do it so well.

YOUNG SHE: Just words. Silly, empty, ugly words, all untrue.

HE: I'll die without her. You can't imagine what that feels like!

YOUNG SHE: Yes I can.

HE: Good. Then I'll see you tonight. To pick up the love letter.

HE leaves. SHE looks at her hand.

YOUNG SHE: What have you done, foolish hand? Foolish, foolish hand.

YOUNG SHE turns toward the person upon whose hand she sits, and leans into them for a moment. ME removes both small marionettes and puts them away. Speaking as SHE, he makes his way back to her. He does not take her in hand, but instead sits on the floor in front of her and the patron holding her as SHE finishes speaking.

SHE: My life did change that day, true, but not in the way I had hoped. Instead, I became the go-to gal for love letters, a strange hobby that soon became a career. Like a black-market Cyrano of sorts, with a panache for prose and a charming command of cursive.

It was a well-kept secret, which served me well when the New Now came to power and erased written language. But though invisible and unseen, I was not unknown, and still I was found.

I added the ceremonies when I knew it would all be lost, never to return. The rituals and rites tonight are not a religion, mine are not the word of God. The words themselves are divine, each a little god unto itself; combined, something holy when speaking to another of one's love. And I, just a disciple, guarding its sacred life, as I write in a still foolish hand.

But enough of that. A walk down memory lane gets you nowhere but up your own ass.

> ME *takes her control from the person who has been holding her.*

Thanks for the hand, honey.

> SHE *addresses the crowd while riding on* ME*'s hand.*

Who has come to have a love letter written?

BOY: *(off)* I have.

SHE: And who are you?

BOY: *(off)* A person . . . who . . . wants a . . . love letter?

> SHE *chuckles.*

SHE: Ah, the hesitant bravura of a nascent Casanova. This'll be fun!

> ME *takes* BOY *from the puppet crate and stands him in front of* SHE *atop the crate.*

You're just a kid. A boy in a man suit.

BOY: I wear it to blend in.

SHE: How's that working out for you?

BOY: Not at all. But I like the suit.

SHE: What's your name?

BOY: We don't use them. Too dangerous. I'm never going in a cage again.

SHE: Are you alone?

BOY: Here, right now? Yes, just me.

SHE: Safe at last.

BOY: I don't feel safe.

SHE: These are friends.

BOY: I'm in love.

SHE: Ah. A lot harder to run from that captor.

BOY: She's amazing. She scares me, which I like, because she's not . . . soft. Beautiful, yes, and a warrior. Stronger than me, more than I could ever be. And she makes me feel, um, really, really stupid.

SHE: Well, Cupid, you little bitch. Bullseye! Have you told her?

BOY: Are you kidding? No way. She'd kill me. But when I heard about you, and the letters, I thought maybe that was a way. You know, because if I gave it to her, she would have to find you to have it read, and then she'd know.

SHE: And you wouldn't be dead. At least not right away.

BOY: What?

SHE: Now I'm kidding. Well, this will be a challenge. Come on, let's go.

BOY: Where?

SHE: Well, I don't write the love letters in public. I may be from carnival blood, but I'm not a sideshow act. No, we go to my tent, you tell me the secrets of your heart, and I write your letter. In private.

> *SHE starts walking away. BOY follows, but indicates the audience.*

BOY: What about them?

SHE: Oh, they'll be fine, they're in Me's hands. He's been telling them a story from the Long Ago and Once Upon a Time. I'm sure there's another chapter coming up.

> *SHE and BOY exit.*

ME: Maestro, music please!

Record Cue #6: Despair

> *ME fastens the puppet belt around his waist, hanging the necessary puppets for the following scene, but performs in the open without the walking stage. ZAKO enters.*

ZAKO: Despair! Disgrace! Disenchantment! Dis road leads absolutely nowhere! I feel like I'm walking in circles. I'm so hungry I could eat my shoe.

> *ME lifts one of his feet, but ZAKO cannot reach it.*

The KING OF THE BIRDS *pops up. He is a man, obviously, but wears a rubber glove atop his head.*

KING: Step right up, friend. Care to see the show?

ZAKO: What show is it?

KING: It's a . . . y'know . . . a good show.

ZAKO: Why would I want to see a good show? I want to see a great show!

KING: Okay, then it's a great show.

ZAKO: That's not what you said. You said it was only good.

KING: But you want great, and the customer is always right.

ZAKO: No they're not. The customers are idiots! You are a terrible busker.

KING: I'm not a busker. I'm a king, see.

ZAKO: Impossible. I am the King! The King of the Carnival! Zako Budaydos, the greatest sideshowman in the world! I have the crown to prove it, see?

KING: Well, I'm a king too. King of the Birds!

ZAKO: You're not a bird. You're a man wearing a chicken hat.

KING: I'm the King of the Birds. Ask anyone in town, on the fair-ground, ask my wife. She's a cockatoo.

ZAKO: I've heard that about her.

KING: So, do you still want to see the show?

ZAKO: No, I don't want to see the show.

KING: Just as well, it's not very good.

ZAKO: Why would you tell me that?

KING: Because it's the truth.

ZAKO: This is why you are a terrible busker. No one who comes to the carnival wants the truth. They want us to lie, they expect us to lie, the most beautiful lies they could never imagine on their own.

ZAKO steps forward, addressing the crowd.

Menses and ladykinds, I invite you to pass by this tent quickly, resisting what exotic temptations may lie within. Yes, friends, turn away, run and flee, for once seen, your lives can never be the same. The peril of parting this curtain is a key to unlocking your own quivering passions, releasing the animal within you! No, gentlewomen and femmymen, I beg of you, do not thrust your coins into my hand simply to see the most thrilling trove of erotic fantasies in this canvas cave of carnal curiosities.

KING: You're hired!

ZAKO: Who said I was looking for a job?

KING: Your growling stomach tipped me off. And the way you looked at my legs.

ZAKO: I do enjoy a nice drumstick.

When do I meet the company? The artists! The acrobats, the dancers and freaks, the musicians and clowns.

KING: Well, there's only one, see.

ZAKO: I'm used to working with a cast of thousands! Okay, maybe hundreds. At least a dozen. But one is enough, I can work with that. And I have a bear suit.

KING: Oh, you don't want to hide this one in a bear suit.

ZAKO: Why not? They love the bear.

KING: Because she's already bare.

ZAKO: She's what? She who?

KING: Miss Willow, the tattooed lady!

As ZAKO speaks, the KING OF THE BIRDS pops down. ZAKO continues, facing out, as behind him MISS WILLOW appears. She is a rod puppet, beautiful and nude, her porcelain skin covered in blue willow china designs.

ZAKO: What? A tattooed lady? What kind of act is that? They don't do anything; they just stand there. No trapeze, no fortune-telling, no death-defying daring-do. Just . . . tattoos. How can I possibly be expected to work with . . .

ZAKO turns and sees MISS WILLOW.

. . . The most beautiful creature in the world.

He giggles nervously. She giggles.

Hello.

She giggles.

I'm Zako.

She giggles.

Zako Budaydos.

She giggles.

You must be Miss Willow. A pleasure to meet you.

He bows. She giggles.

I'm the new busker. We're going to be together. I mean, a team, um, working together.

She giggles.

Do you only giggle?

WILLOW: No, but you make me laugh.

ZAKO: Because of the way I look.

WILLOW: No, because of the way you look at me.

ZAKO: You are the most beautiful sight I've ever seen.

WILLOW: I am not so. More like you than you know.

ZAKO: I am a humpbacked freak.

WILLOW: I thought you were a king.

ZAKO: Now you make me laugh.

WILLOW: You're wearing a crown.

ZAKO: An old tin can, cut down and bent, like the beaten dog who wears it, begging at the feet of a goddess.

WILLOW: In the sideshow, I am special, exotic, unique. But no one wants different in the light of day. Only at night and when they pay. You see? Like you. A freak.

ZAKO: No, a queen. You excite me . . . and not in a weird way.

WILLOW: Really?

ZAKO: Okay, maybe a little weird.

She giggles.

WILLOW: I'm not used to standing outside the tent. It's chilly.

ZAKO: I have a fur coat to warm you.

WILLOW: Mink?

ZAKO: No.

WILLOW: Chinchilla?

ZAKO: No.

WILLOW: Beaver?

ZAKO: Stop it.

WILLOW: Ocelot? Leopard? Fox?

ZAKO: Nope, nope, and nope.

WILLOW: Then what?

ZAKO: Bear.

WILLOW: Really?

ZAKO: Sort of.

WILLOW: Did you kill it yourself?

ZAKO: It's a long story.

WILLOW: You could just hold me.

ZAKO: I could, but there's a danger.

WILLOW: How so?

ZAKO: I may never let go.

WILLOW: Well, you did say we're a team now.

ZAKO: You wouldn't think it weird?

WILLOW: Perhaps a little.

ZAKO: Perhaps I shouldn't.

WILLOW: Perhaps it's meant to be.

ZAKO: You are an angel.

WILLOW: And you are . . .

ZAKO: An idiot.

WILLOW: King of the Idiots.

ZAKO: Without a throne.

WILLOW: Then claim your seat at last. Come home.

He goes to embrace her.

King Zako?

ZAKO: Miss Willow?

WILLOW: Not in front of the punters.

He embraces MISS WILLOW, who giggles as they are put away in the crate.

ME puts on a handpuppet of SHE. ME's fingers are exposed as her hands.

SHE: Me, what am I doing?

ME: The next ceremony.

Together ME and SHE produce a basin.

SHE: You filled it?

ME: Yes, see?

SHE: Vodka or gin?

ME: Champagne!

SHE: Really?

ME: Of course not.

SHE: Then what?

ME: Water.

SHE: Fuck.

She looks in the basin.

What's that?

ME: An orange.

SHE: Why?

ME: You asked for it.

SHE: I asked for orange blossoms to perfume the bath, asshole. This is a rind, the peel, the skin.

ME: In the water, giving it scent.

SHE: What were you thinking?

ME: I think we're on the run and underground. It's a miracle I found an orange at all.

SHE: Yes, we're in the shit.

ME: So squint and smell.

She inhales.

SHE: Ah, orange blossoms.

ME: All rise for the Ceremony of the Lost Words.

SHE: Oh, let them sit, Me, they've been up and down all night like a groom's cock.

They scan the crowd, wandering among them.

Self-adjust, move around if you want or must. I'm going to stay put, right . . .

Settling on one person in the audience, SHE *touches their cheek.*

. . . here. Dear one, you are found, to assist with the Lost Words! But before you step on hallowed ground, you must be washed. Someone bring a chair for our novitiate.

A chair is brought. SHE *commands the person.*

Sit. And, sweetheart, take off your shoes and socks.

ME *and* SHE *kneel in front of the person, placing the basin on the floor.* ME *hands a washcloth to* SHE.

Trust me. I am your servant.

SHE wets the cloth in the basin. ME holds out his hand.

Trust me.

SHE guides the foot into ME's hand. The stage manager starts the music.

Record Cue #7: Foot Washing

During the following, SHE slowly and gently washes the feet of the person, ME cradling their feet in his hand one at a time.

SHE: In the Before, when free passage was still allowed and art had not yet been banned or burned or plundered, I saw her. The *Mona Lisa*. And she smiled just for me. But I did not take her home to live above my sofa. Nor would the ceiling of the Sistine Chapel ever be over my bed, any more than the Trevi Fountain would be my bathtub.

You don't own beauty. You love it. That's all. You love it knowing it's not yours, though once seen, is part of you forever. I learned my lesson well. Make your peace, unbeautiful one. It will not love you back. Make your peace. I made mine, loving a beautiful man who would never love me in return. I am unloved, true. But I loved, truly. That is a kind of beauty too.

And yet, you are here. So I shall close my eyes for a moment and pretend you walked toward me, your chosen, shuddering like a girl again, as I bathe in the beauty.

SHE lays her head on the person's foot for a moment.

Music out. SHE rises, bows, and takes their hand.

Now stand and take my hand, you're ready to enter the sacred space.

ME removes the basin of water and the handpuppet of SHE.

He gets a marionette of SHE. Her costume is elaborate, bizarre, yet spare. A hoop cage skirt onto which are fastened small pieces of paper.

The stage manager puts on the next record.

Record Cue #8: Invitation

SHE: The words upon my frock are from the past: poets, playwrights, dreamers, prophets, cons, and fools. Let them remind you what it is to be alive.

My darling chosen one, now you may kneel before me.

They kneel in front of the chair, SHE standing on the seat in front of them.

Pluck a piece of paper from my ghostly gown. I do not know or care which you'll choose, any one will do.

Then hand it up to Me.

They hand the paper to ME, who studies it for a moment.

Hands together, palms up, place them on the chair.

They do so, and SHE carefully steps onto their hands.

Darling, you are the dais upon which I'll give my recitation. Raise your hands, slowly, surely, without hesitation. Steady, higher, a little more, there. Stay still and hold me, I know you will. I trust you. I am in your hands now, beautiful one. Don't let me down.

Friends, I give you now, a passage from . . . Which one are we doing, Me?

ME shows her the piece of paper.

Ah, marvellous! A favourite of mine. Well done, hon.

Tonight's recitation is a passage from . . .

SHE names the author or source.

Well? Begin, Me.

ME: I can't read this.

SHE: Of course you can.

ME: No, it's too small.

SHE: It's the same it's always been.

ME: But I'm not.

SHE: Oh for fuck's sake. Way to kill a ceremony mood, Me!

Music out.

Does anyone have a pair of reading glasses or bifocals they can put on my old fool here? If so, come forward now, even though we haven't washed your feet.

Someone from the audience puts their glasses on ME. SHE begins to recite a passage as he reads, either Whitman, Shakespeare, Rumi, Keats, Gibran, the Bible, or, most probably, a dirty limerick. The recitation finished, SHE leans in close to the kneeling person's face.

I will not lie to you, my beautiful one, I would like to stay here, raised up by you forever. But I suspect you'd like to put your shoes on and disappear into the crowd from whence you came, far from the claws of a chattering crone. So, let me down gently, love, and I will let you go.

They lower their hands and SHE *steps off.*

Goodbye. And thank you. And, hon, give these glasses back.

They stand, take the glasses from ME, *and rejoin the others.*

ME *puts the marionette of* SHE *away.*

Record Cue #9: Zako Show

ME: Friends, move around and stretch your legs, and raise your Others once again, and by the symbols on the back of their clothes, create three communities, please. Red circles cluster here, blue triangles over here, and yellow squares gather there.

As the groups form, ME *puts the handpuppet of* ZAKO *on his hand, who bursts into the crowd, interacting with the groups of Others.*

ZAKO: Ladies, gentlemen, and Others all, pups and gals, friends and pals, dames and swells, mams and sirs, hims and hers and thems, and all of you, it's true, it's me, the one and only Zako Budaydos!

I hear your whispers, "Zako, where's the tent, where's the show?" Aha, it's true, the carnival is not here. Yet! I'm doing a bit of advance work, snooping around to see which town would be the best to fleece—er—play. And now that posters and handbills are suppressed, I thought it best to avoid the written word completely and speak to you in person, sweetly from my heart.

I have heard Red Circle City is a delight, and I can see why. Everyone's so gorgeous, handsome, pretty! I'm a lucky guy. Tell me, miss, is this your sister? What? Your daughter? No, impossible! If I had a leg, you'd be pulling it! Listen, for you, a special deal. Come to the show, I'll charge you full price! Bring a friend, I'll charge you twice! No, no, no, no, no need to thank me. I'm just nice.

I've been told Blue Triangle Town is where the action is. And I can see why. Look at this guy! Handsome, strong, and smart. So if we play your town, you should bring this fine lady in her delightful gown. And also too, this sweet lad. Why not? The carnival is a freak show, what better place to get your freak on too. Come once, then come again, for I guarantee, my friend, the road to heaven isn't paved at all! It's filthy.

But, let me not forget the denizens of Yellow Square, for there, I hear, are people so grand, and wise, and just a little odd. But in my little tent, you are a god! Come and see the show, and know it's all for you.

But sadly, these towns in which you live are far too small.

Why do you live in separate states, divided by triangles, circles, and squares, told that our colours must keep us apart? Come together, sisters and brothers. Shake hands, say hello. There's strength in numbers, and the bigger the town, the bigger my take, and more of you to con—er—to convince that I, Zako Budaydos, am the greatest showman! For now, goodbye, but I shall return and pitch my tent for you, and you, and you, here in Otherland.

ZAKO bows grandly and walks away. ME addresses the audience.

ME: Be seated, if you want. Wander if you will. Zako's going home, be still. Be still.

ME grabs the rod puppet of MISS WILLOW. The following scene is played in the open.

ZAKO: Surprise!

WILLOW: You're back!

ZAKO: Nothing could keep me away.

WILLOW: I missed you, it seemed so long.

ZAKO: Mere days, a week at most, but now I'm here to stay.

WILLOW: Did you find a town for us to play?

ZAKO: I found three and made them into one!

WILLOW: My clever little king. I have a surprise for you. Actually, two.

ZAKO: That you look at me at all is the greatest surprise.

WILLOW: I've written you a love letter.

ZAKO: No.

WILLOW: It's true.

ZAKO: Oh no.

WILLOW: What's wrong?

ZAKO: On my travels to find a town, I kept my ear close to the ground for whisperings and news. The dumbing of the people by the authorities is in full swing.

WILLOW: Surely it will bring even more gullible punters our way.

ZAKO: You don't understand. Words are dangerous now.

WILLOW: But what harm is a love letter?

ZAKO: That's where we share our secrets. And they don't want us to have words of our own. Only the ones they condone. Whisper your secrets to my ear, and I'll hold them in my heart. But you must destroy the letter.

WILLOW: I cannot.

She stands in front of him. Slowly she turns, showing writing tattooed on her back.

ZAKO: What have you done?

WILLOW: If I cover myself with words of love, can you read between the lines?

ZAKO: For all to see.

WILLOW: But secret too.

ZAKO reads aloud.

ZAKO: "My Omi,
I am a billy doo,
my love written
on my eek,

my oyster,
my willets,
my all
To be held in your
Lappers and read by
you."

WILLOW: I told you I had two surprises. The carnival will have a prince or princess, my little king.

ZAKO: You must marry me!

WILLOW: No, it's not necessary, Zako.

ZAKO: Yes, it is!

WILLOW: Not at all.

ZAKO: It's the only thing to do!

WILLOW: Says who?

ZAKO: Me, I do. Zako Budaydos, the ugly little dwarf, broken, beaten, and bent. Yet an angel loves me, so I stand tall, because Heaven extended its hand. And this news, I am a giant now. I will never be normal, but this must be how it feels to be unbroken and unbent. Marry me.

WILLOW: But how? Who would marry two freaks from the tent?

ZAKO: I know a guy . . . with a chicken hat.

WILLOW: The King of the Birds?

ZAKO: I'll ask him to preside.

WILLOW: It's absurd.

ZAKO: It's the sideshow, my love! So, will you be my bride?

WILLOW: Yes.

ZAKO: And trust me?

WILLOW: Forever.

ZAKO: Then please, you have to get covered and hide. These written words cannot be seen by anyone other than me.

WILLOW: They were only ever meant for you. But where to hide?

ZAKO: In plain view.

WILLOW: I don't understand.

ZAKO: Your betrothed is a carny, master of the sleight of hand. Miss Willow, you've made a career being bare on display, but what if today, you become the bear?

WILLOW: Zako Budaydos and His Dancing Bear!

ZAKO: Okay?

WILLOW: Okay.

ZAKO: Just one thing. The bear costume may be slightly cursed, so when you're wearing it, be rehearsed and try not to be an idiot.

WILLOW: I'll do my best.

ZAKO: Good. Now, go get dressed.

She starts to leave, but pauses and turns.

WILLOW: Zako?

ZAKO: Hmmm?

WILLOW: What about our wedding?

ZAKO: It will be the most joyous celebration!

WILLOW: But I can't be there.

ZAKO: Hmmm, true. So, I marry the bear! Think of the publicity!

WILLOW: Now who's being an idiot?

ZAKO: My love, it's the carnival. And the more bizarre, the more they'll pay. Trust me. What could possibly go wrong?

ZAKO laughs gleefully as they exit.

ME places an envelope on top of the crate, then takes marionettes of BOY IN THE MAN SUIT and WARRIOR GURL in hand, standing them on either side of the envelope.

BOY: Hey.

She turns, startled.

GURL: Don't ever sneak up on me. I could have killed you.

BOY: Sorry, I forgot.

GURL: Forgetting gets you dead.

He indicates the letter on the ground between them.

BOY: That's for you.

GURL: What is it?

BOY: A letter.

GURL: Are you trying to get us both killed now? I can't walk around with that. Who is it from?

BOY: Me. It's how I feel. About you.

GURL: Don't be stupid.

BOY: I can't help it. The letter tells you why.

GURL: Why don't you just tell me?

BOY: I did. There. In the letter. Read it.

GURL: No.

BOY: Please.

GURL: I said no!

BOY: Why not?

GURL: Because I can't read.

BOY: Good, then we're the same.

GURL: That doesn't make us the same. It just means we're like everyone now. Where did you get this?

BOY: The Keeper of the Lost Hand.

GURL: No way.

BOY: It's true. I just met her once, for this. I told her things.

GURL: What things?

BOY: Things about you.

GURL: Do you really want me to punch you?

BOY: Kind of. Yes.

GURL: What?

BOY: Look, I told her things so she could write the letter!

GURL: They'll find her now, because of you.

BOY: She moves around. Every night, somewhere new.

GURL: How did you find her?

BOY: I followed them.

He indicates the audience.

They have a look in their eyes.

He looks at the crowd.

Can you feel it?

GURL: I feel stupid.

BOY: That's what it feels like. So, will you have the letter read?

GURL: If it mentions my breasts, you're dead.

BOY: I'm pretty sure I didn't bring them up, but the old lady is pretty wild, so I can't promise anything.

GURL: How do I find her?

BOY: Follow them. They'll lead the way.

> *The marionettes of* BOY *and* GURL *are put away.* ME *wheels out a three-tiered dais.* SHE *is on top, standing in front of a cardboard throne. There is an envelope on the ground.*
>
> *The stage manager puts on a record.*

Record Cue #10: Chicken

SHE: Someone gave me a chicken once.
Thankfully, it was dead.
I'm not sure the chicken was so grateful.
In those first days when the Before was final
And the New Now in flight,
A pilgrim to my camp might thrust a useless coin
Or a redundant bill into my hand as thanks.
Because we only knew how to pay.
That was the way of the old days.
We hadn't a clue how high the price would be
In the cruel currency ahead.

I had a chicken once,
Plucked and pasty, a harbinger of
My own future flesh.
I thrust my hand into its empty cavity,
Thinking how lucky that bird was.
Dead.
Unfeeling.
Uncaring.

Spared the humiliation of knowing
My unwelcome hand was there.

I had a chicken once,
Roasted but unstuffed.
I had no appetite but ate her anyway.
That pullet was payment for words,
Words of love.
Appropriate, I think.
Sometimes love makes you
Devour
Yourself.
But that's the price you pay
If you're a chicken.

Music out.

Our ceremony continues with the Reading Rites. If any of you seekers have in your possession a letter, delivered solely to your hand, you may now step forward to have it read.

ME *stands a marionette of a man on the lower tier. He is handsome in a rough way, not well dressed, perhaps a labourer.*

GUY: I have one of your letters.

SHE: They are never mine.

GUY: But in your hand. So, yours.

SHE: And you know the one who delivered it?

GUY: Yes.

SHE: Then it's yours.

GUY: But it's a love letter.

SHE: That's what I do, baby.

GUY: I didn't ask for it.

SHE: Of course not. You don't request a love letter. It's a gift.

GUY: It's not right.

SHE: You're not worthy of love? Of the sacrifice someone made to find me, to take the letter and deliver it? She made an epic journey for you, wouldn't you agree?

GUY: He, not she.

SHE: I see.

GUY: You do?

SHE: I see no difference. The effort was great, all the same, perhaps that particular journey to you even more heroic.

GUY: I need you to read it.

SHE: Then be seated.

GUY: Just read it.

SHE: My ceremony, my rules. Sit.

He sits reluctantly.

I need a pilgrim to help me, someone to open the envelope and hold the letter while I read.

SHE either selects someone or a volunteer joins her. They hold the letter in front of her.

Me, did I write this?

ME looks at the letter and nods.

GUY: Is there a problem?

SHE: You tell me.

GUY: What do you mean?

SHE: When you see this man, how do you greet him?

GUY: I clench my hand into a fist and never look him in the eye.

SHE: That's why. Greater than usual danger was implied. I remember this one now.

GUY: So read it.

SHE: You won't understand it.

GUY: Read.

SHE reads.

SHE: "Omi, my omi. Forgive this billy doo, but every time I feel you ajax, my thumping cheat soars. I know your ogles are turned by the palones, but I could be benar in a bijou lattie by ourselves. Let me worship at your plates, work my way up your lallies, look into your minces, and pleasure you more than any dolly palone could. I heart your eek, the damp dark riah on your bulging thews, the scar on the back of your lils which makes me weak at the lalls. The best dish ever served to an omi palone like me who longs to be your bona dolly molly. Oh omi, my omi."

GUY: Why do you speak gibberish?

SHE: I read exactly what's written. It's code. A secret language.

GUY: What language?

SHE: Polari.

GUY: From where?

SHE: Everywhere. Gypsies, sailors, prostitutes, and Punch and Judy men, the circus and fairgrounds, the theatre, Yiddish and Cockney slang, and this version, the secret tongue of homosexuals in the Before. Polari comes from Parlyaree, the cant of my birthplace. The carnival.

GUY: He knows I'm not that way. Why would he do this?

SHE: It's just love, honey. Tell him you're flattered.

GUY: But I'm not.

SHE: Then why are you here? You could have rejected the letter outright; you could have tossed it away. Instead, you found me, because you wanted to hear his words.

GUY: Of course I did. It's about me!

SHE: So vanity propelled you here.

GUY: I didn't ask for this!

SHE: Neither did he. Love just happens. No one's to blame.

Let's wrap this up.

GUY: Fine by me.

SHE: Others, all rise, and fix your eyes upon this recipient in witness of his answer. Do you accept these words of love?

GUY: No, I can't.

SHE: My friends, the letter is rejected. I'm afraid the Reading Rites ceremony is done for tonight.

GUY: So that's it?

SHE: I can't change your heart, any more than you can deny him his.

GUY: What happens now?

SHE: Nothing. Nothing at all. You may go.

He starts to leave, then pauses and turns to SHE.

GUY: Look, I . . . I just don't want it.

SHE: I understand.

GUY: Do you?

SHE: More than you know, pal.

GUY *exits.* ME *removes* SHE *and the throne.*

ME: She is going to rest, but we have another ceremony now, the best. For today is the day in the Long Ago when Zako Budaydos marries his bear.

Maestro, music, please!

This calls for a cake, don't you think?

Record Cue #11: Wedding

ME *covers the dais with a cloth covering. It is muslin, like* ZAKO*'s stage and the clothing of the Others, trimmed in wide pink rick rack like frosting piping.*

ME *places* MISS WILLOW *on top of the cake. She wears the bear suit in a wedding dress. He places the bear head over hers.*

ME: Others, rise!

As the music ends, ME *produces the* KING OF THE BIRDS *and* ZAKO.

KING: Dearly beloved, and the rest of ya, we are gathered here today to witness the union of this guy, Zako Budaydos . . .

ZAKO: That's me! I'm the King of the Carnival!

KING: The man who stole the heart of my only attraction, Miss . . .

ZAKO: Uh uh uh!

KING: I mean, stole the heart of this bear. Yeah, this bear, see. And what a lovely gal she is. A great cuddler, not a picky eater, plus she brings her own fur coat.

ZAKO: And she can dance!

WILLOW: Not now, Zako, please hurry.

ZAKO: Let's move this along.

KING: Do you, Zako Budaydos, take this woman . . .

ZAKO: Bear.

KING: Yeah, this bear, see, to be your wife?

ZAKO: I do.

KING: And do you, Miss . . . bear, take this man to be your husband?

MISS WILLOW *moans inside the bear suit.*

WILLOW: Zako, I think the baby is coming.

ZAKO: Speed it up!

KING: By the power vested in me, because I'm King of the Birds, see, I now pronounce you man and wife. You may kiss the bride, or whatever you do with a bear.

ZAKO and MISS WILLOW embrace.

ME: Maestro, music please!

Record Cue #12: Dance Party

ZAKO: My friends! Everybody dance!

The KING OF THE BIRDS is put away and ZAKO is raised high, indicating for the audience and their Others to do the same. MISS WILLOW is laid down on top of the cake. A joyful all-audience dance party ensues. It should be long enough to encourage some abandon and dancing around the space.

At the height of the dance party, ME blows a whistle, piercing the music.

BILLYSCHTICK appears.

BILLYSCHTICK: Stop the music!

Music out.

Silence! Stop that dancing, all of you! Who is responsible for this?

He approaches one of the Others.

Is it you? Silence!

He approaches another, and then another.

You? Quiet! Or perhaps you, yes?

ZAKO: Excuse me, sir. The party is mine.

BILLYSCHTICK: And who are you?

ZAKO: I'm Zako Budaydos! And you are?

BILLYSCHTICK: My name is Billyschtick.

ZAKO: Pleased to meet you, Mr. Billyschtick.

BILLYSCHTICK: Constable Billyschtick! I am the authority in this region.

ZAKO: I am the King of the Carnival! And this is my queen.

BILLYSCHTICK: This is a bear.

ZAKO: This is my bride.

BILLYSCHTICK: You married a bear?

ZAKO: It's a long story.

BILLYSCHTICK: What do you take me for?

ZAKO: An idiot?

MISS WILLOW moans.

BILLYSCHTICK: What's wrong with the bear?

ZAKO: She's emotional. It's her wedding day! And she's overcome with joy to see all our friends.

BILLYSCHTICK: So, these people are your friends?

ZAKO: Of course!

BILLYSCHTICK: What are their names?

ZAKO: Why?

BILLYSCHTICK: So I can report them!

ZAKO: Ah. Well, sadly, I don't know.

BILLYSCHTICK: You don't know their names?

ZAKO: How could I? We just met.

BILLYSCHTICK: But you said you were friends.

ZAKO: Do you have friends?

BILLYSCHTICK: No. I have power.

ZAKO: But if you did have friends, what would their names be?

BILLYSCHTICK: I don't know!

ZAKO: See? We're exactly the same! Neither of us knows our friend's names.

MISS WILLOW moans.

BILLYSCHTICK: Silence the bear, I can't think!

ZAKO: Yes, that's obvious.

MISS WILLOW moans.

BILLYSCHTICK: I said silence her!

MISS WILLOW moans.

WILLOW: Zako, the baby . . . it's coming.

BILLYSCHTICK: I will not be threatened by a wild animal.

ZAKO: She's not dangerous. She's in pain.

BILLYSCHTICK: Then put her out of her misery.

ZAKO: What?

BILLYSCHTICK: You heard me.

ZAKO: No!

BILLYSCHTICK: Then I will.

ZAKO: Please, no, you can't.

BILLYSCHTICK: You're right. Someone else will do the deed.

ZAKO: No!

BILLYSCHTICK singles out two audience members and hands them the puppet of ZAKO.

BILLYSCHTICK: You two, hold him back. Do not let go.

BILLYSCHTICK has produced a club from the shelf inside the cake. ME walks through the crowd as BILLYSCHTICK slowly makes his choice. He offers the club to one of the Others, addressing the puppet only, not the person holding it.

You. Take this club in your hands. Now beat the bear. Well? What are you waiting for? Beat the bear! Do it! Silence the bear. Beat her!

Why do you hesitate? There is no place for weakness now!

He grabs the puppet by the neck and pulls it quickly from the audience member, leaving their hand bare. He focuses on another and offers them the club.

MISS WILLOW *moans.*

Beat this sickly beast until it cries no more!

He grabs the Other as before, leaving the audience member's hand bare, and moves to another. He offers them the club.

What of you? Cowardice or domination?

He grabs the Other, disposing of it.

Look at you. Delicate . . .

Another is taken.

. . . fragile . . .

Another.

. . . soft.

He darts through the crowd, randomly snatching puppets off hands. It is frenzied, angry. He stops, again offering the club to one of the Others.

A culling is necessary to ensure continuation of the strong. Embrace the power of your privilege. Beat the bear.

MISS WILLOW moans loudly.

Do it!

MISS WILLOW moans, louder. BILLYSCHTICK throws the lifeless Others into their crate.

Do it!

MISS WILLOW moans. BILLYSCHTICK walks back to her, standing over her. He holds the club up, offering it to the audience.

Last chance. Beat the bear.

He raises the club as MISS WILLOW screams in pain.

Do you think I enjoy this? If you only knew. I love it.

He strikes her with the club, beating repeatedly and violently, punctuated by the whistle.

There is finally silence. A moment of stillness. BILLYSCHTICK slowly regards the audience.

None of you did what you were told, but all of you did what was expected. Nothing. Nothing at all. This is why you're so easy to control.

BILLYSCHTICK leaves. ME retrieves ZAKO, placing him on his hand again. ZAKO removes the bear head, revealing MISS WILLOW's face.

ZAKO: Willow. Willow, my love.

WILLOW: Zako.

ZAKO: I failed you.

WILLOW: No.

ZAKO: I am a little man.

WILLOW: You are a king.

ZAKO: I did not protect you.

WILLOW: Zako, look inside.

ZAKO: I see only my shame.

WILLOW: No, you idiot. The bear suit, look.

Slowly, ZAKO lifts the skirt of the wedding dress, revealing a baby nestled on MISS WILLOW's belly.

ZAKO: I don't know what to do.

WILLOW: Survive.

ZAKO: Without you, I am not alive.

WILLOW: Me, I am weak. Just once, please, could we let the Others speak?

ME nods and addresses the crowd.

ME: I'll whisper Willow's words into your ear, and you will say them loudly, so they will live in Zako's heart, proud and clear. You, beloved ones, are her last breath.

He slowly wanders through the crowd, cradling MISS WILLOW and ZAKO, pausing to whisper the following into various audience member's ears, line by line. The break for each new person is indicated by a forward slash.

WILLOW/ME/AUDIENCE: Remember the tale
Of the Knight in Shining Armour? /
You are mine, little man, /
In your tin can crown. /
Forever shining bright. /
But now, you are she
And I am he, /
Drowning
Into the light. /
I give you this flower,
Our child. /
Teach her all the words
And give her the power /
To keep our love alive.

MISS WILLOW continues alone and aloud.

WILLOW: Zako.
Zako, my king.
Forget me not.

He kisses her; she dies. ZAKO rests his head on her breast, his arm around the baby. He lifts his head, slowly looking at the entire audience.

ZAKO: Not one of you stepped forward.

ME carries them away.

Record Cue #13: Childhood

ME has placed a small figure on his hand, his index and middle fingers becoming the legs of a child, dressed like a fairy. She dances atop the dais.

ME: Zako disappeared; a phantom, a fugitive, a father deep in the forest, fearful for his fairy princess. She, whose only subjects were the trees and flowers, streams and mushroom thrones, and the breeze that lifted her above the terra incognita exile.

But one day, when it was time for her to stop flying and learn to stand, invisible like you, hidden in plain view, Zako delivered her into the hands of another mother named Superior. Nature was scrubbed and beaten out of her, replaced by God's endless words.

ME stops animating her and his hands come together in prayer.

She kept a whisper of the language of her parents locked inside her mind to help her read between the lines. And a memory of buried treasure; her father's crown, lying in state in a woodland grave, waiting to be unearthed by She, the future queen, at her coronation of madness.

Music out.

He puts the child puppet away.

SHE enters. Now simply a small head of her on ME's index finger, his bare hand exposed as her fingers.

SHE: I'm going to dance with my mother today.

SHE flitters her fingernails in ME's face.

I'm a mess.

ME: You're beautiful.

SHE: My mother was beautiful. Painted like a china teacup.

ME pulls out a small bottle of nail polish from his pocket.

ME: Then let's paint you too.

SHE: Oh honey, yes, please!

SHE looks at the colour of the bottle.

Blue Willow?

ME: Forget-me-not blue. Let's paint a bouquet on those nails.

SHE: A bouquet from a friend is always welcome.

SHE kisses ME on the cheek.

But a bouquet from a lover is better.

ME: Then let's find you one.

His free hand gestures across the audience.

Choose.

ME walks with her as SHE looks at the audience. SHE stops in front of one man. ME hands the bottle of nail polish to him as SHE offers her fingers to the man.

SHE: Paint my fingernails, please.

ME and SHE kneel or sit beside the man as he paints her nails.

All the memories of my life are in these fingers. Picking strawberries, building sandcastles, scrubbing the filth of life from my flesh, writing love letters. And one letter, thrust from these foolish fingers into the hands of an ordinary man who simply didn't want me.

I have never spoken those words aloud. But I must now. To release them into air, unjoined and separate again, ready to be of service to the next breath of longing.

Record Cue #14: Love Letter

SHE recites her love letter as her nails continue to be painted.

SHE: If the moon whispered, "You may have your true love, but you must share him with me," I would say, "Fine, I shall live without moonlight, for he is mine alone." If the stars were to coo, "He is ours too," then I would live without the constellations—my love the only map to find my way home to you. And should God command, "He is thine, but you must choose between he and Me," then I would say, "Devil, be gone," for only the divine could let me see, and love, and worship you.

The four fingers painted, SHE leans into the man as if to kiss him, then stops herself.

You mustn't kiss me . . .

This is the mouth of a liar.

SHE whispers into the man's ear.

I lied.

SHE pulls back, opening her confession to the congregation.

I lied. Before, when I said my love was true. I don't love him now. It's been a forever since I did. I'm a liar for keeping up this bullshit, reciting girlish moon and stars drivel about a man. Excuse me from love's banquet please, I'm far too full of starving!

I was a little disappointed. I vowed to love him forever, to keep this, history's greatest one-sided romance, alive! Like a fucking nun of love, married to my mythical deity.

And like all true martyrs, I spent my whole life pretending, carrying my sad, dead love inside me like an unexpelled miscarriage.

I'm a fucking saint. Crucified by my own foolish hand . . .

SHE turns, face to face with ME.

. . . and the mouth of a liar.

SHE turns back to the man.

But you leave me with something beautiful on my crippled hand. For that, I thank you, extraordinary man.

SHE touches his face gently for a moment, ME's hand caressing his cheek. Turning away, SHE leans into ME, causing him to arch back.

Why did you do this to me?

ME: You were a story to tell.

SHE: You could have just written it down.

ME looks at the audience.

ME: But then they wouldn't have come.

SHE sighs.

SHE: I'm done, Me.

> *ME removes the small head of SHE from his finger and puts the first handpuppet version of her in the hooded robe on his hand.*

You have to let me go.

ME: I know.

SHE: You'll be alone.

ME: I have friends.

SHE: Bullshit.

ME: It's true.

SHE: Who?

ME: A funny little dwarf. And a man with a chicken hat.

SHE: It's a rubber glove, asshole.

ME: And there's a bear.

SHE: My mother was a bear. I slept in her skin.

Now, ten more words, please.

ME: There isn't time.

SHE: Ten lost words, quickly. Before I'm gone.

> *ME furrows his brow, thinking.*

ME: Effulgent. Capricious. Impetus. Supple. Vignette.

SHE: Wonderful. More.

ME: There's no time.

SHE: Five more.

ME: Whammy.

SHE: Gorgeous!

ME: Cauterize. Didactic. Rendezvous.

SHE: Well done, you. One more. Make it your best.

ME: Hullabaloo!

SHE: Glorious. I knew you were the one, Me. The Keeper of the Lost Hand to be.

ME: No, not me.

SHE: Why not?

ME: I can't pull off a crown.

SHE: Bullshit. You were born to it, you old queen.

ME: I don't want to write love letters.

SHE: Then don't. Just tell the truth. These days, that's the sweetest poetry of all. Teach those warrior children our secret language in cursive code. They'll need it, as they write their own history. Understood?

ME nods.

Good. Now, I have to dance. Maestro, music, please.

Record Cue #15: Waltz

ME reveals the bear puppet on his other hand. It bows to her and extends a hand. SHE curtsies and they dance, ME twirling with them. The puppets embrace as the music slows. ME slowly removes his hand from SHE as the bear cradles her. ME puts the puppets in the One Hundred Handpuppets crate.

ME: There is another story about forget-me-nots. A legend without romantic love, but love nevertheless.

After He had created the earth, God went to every plant and animal and gave them a name. As he finished and was about to leave, He heard a small voice at his feet. "What about me?"

Looking down, He saw, there on the ground, a tiny flower of pale blue hue. It cried, "Oh Lord, I beg you, forget me not!" And God bent down and said to the little plant who had been overlooked, unseen, and ignored, "Because I forgot you once, I will never forget you again. And that shall be your name."

Forget me not.

My name is . . .

Hers.

He indicates the other puppets.

Theirs.

Yours and all the Others.

I am everyone else's story. That's the story of Me.

Tell me a story of you.

He approaches one person, extends his hand to them.

I'm Me. Tell me your name.

When they've said their name, he approaches another, hand extended.

I'm Me. Who are you?

He repeats this a few more times, then finds one last person.

I'm Me.

When they've said their name, he repeats it.

Hello, *(their name).*

He takes a pen from his pocket, kneels before the person, and gives it to them.

Do you remember how to write joined words? Please, write it here.

He offers the underside of his forearm, motioning for them to write on it.

Write your name.

They write on his arm.

See? You're part of me now.

He gestures to the pen in their hand.

Keep it. Do something dangerous with it, *(their name)*. Write a love letter.

I will remember you for . . . the rest of the night.

He walks to the record player and puts on the last record.

Record Cue #16: Finale

ME stands, back to the audience, and listens to the music. He takes one of the pink opera gloves from the FALSE SHE opening costume and puts it on, extending his arm slowly and sensually into handpuppet pose. He turns.

ME: I have to go. So I need the puppets back. Please don't steal them, it makes this untrue if you do. It's not that they're mine. They're me.

He raises his hand in handpuppet pose again.

But now you know how to rise up.

So, say goodbye to your Other, and take them home.

He points to the puppet crate. The audience rise and return their puppets.

ME puts on the FALSE SHE costume. When most of the Others have been put away, ME covers his head with the hood and veil, walks to the exit doors, and exits into the street. He gets into a waiting taxi as the audience watches. It drives away into the night.

The End

Ronnie Burkett has been captivated by puppetry since the age of seven and began touring his shows around Alberta at the age of fourteen. Ronnie Burkett Theatre of Marionettes was formed in 1986, continuously playing on Canada's major stages and as a guest company on numerous tours abroad. Ronnie has received the 2009 Siminovitch Prize in Theatre, the Herbert Whittaker Drama Bench Award for Outstanding Contribution to Canadian Theatre, a *Village Voice* OBIE Award, and four Citations of Excellence from the American Center of the Union Internationale de la Marionnette. In 2019, Ronnie Burkett was appointed as an Officer of the Order of Canada. *Forget Me Not* is the fourteenth production from Ronnie Burkett Theatre of Marionettes, following the international successes *Penny Plain*, *Billy Twinkle*, *10 Days on Earth*, *Provenance*, and the Memory Dress Trilogy of *Tinka's New Dress*, *Street of Blood*, and *Happy*. *The Daisy Theatre*, Ronnie's wildly popular and ever-changing marionette vaudeville show, and the Daisy Christmas show, *Little Dickens*, continue touring to great acclaim. Ronnie lives in Toronto, and from his studio (known in puppetry circles as Puppetland) he continues to imagine and create new work.